Y0-EKP-790

MATH
at Home
It's Everyplace You Are!

Grade 1

Published by Frank Schaffer Publications
an imprint of

McGraw Hill **Children's Publishing**

Editor: Sara Bierling

Mc Graw Hill **Children's Publishing**

Published by Frank Schaffer Publications
An imprint of McGraw-Hill Children's Publishing
Copyright © 2004 McGraw-Hill Children's Publishing

All Rights Reserved • Printed in the United States of America

Limited Reproduction Permission: Permission to duplicate these materials is limited to the person for whom they are purchased. Reproduction for an entire school or school district is unlawful and strictly prohibited.

Send all inquiries to:
McGraw-Hill Children's Publishing
3195 Wilson Drive NW
Grand Rapids, Michigan 49544

Math at Home—It's Everyplace You Are—grade 1
ISBN: 0-7682-2901-4

1 2 3 4 5 6 7 8 9 MAL 09 08 07 06 05 04

The McGraw·Hill Companies

Math at Home—It's Everyplace You Are
Grade 1
Table of Contents

© McGraw-Hill Children's Publishing

0-7682-2901-4 *Math at Home—It's Everyplace You Are*

Math at Home—It's Everyplace You Are

The *It's Everyplace You Are* series makes school curriculum come alive. Engaging, hands-on activities help students see the connection between math concepts and their own experiences. The activities are relevant to students' daily lives, drawing on locations, sounds, and materials that appear in or around familiar surroundings.

This book includes six units to provide a variety of math experiences. Each unit includes reading comprehension exercises, hands-on activities, and written exercises or patterns.

In the Kitchen

In the Neighborhood

On the Porch

In the Bathroom

In the Garage

In Other Places at Home

Meeting the Standards

This book has been designed to meet National Council of Teachers of Mathematics (NCTM) standards. The activities help students learn and practice math concepts and properties. The activities incorporate reading comprehension with math skills such as number concepts, computation, patterning, geometry, problem solving, and data analysis. Plus, each unit provides hands-on learning through cutting, coloring, mazes, and more.

Suggestions for Classroom Use

Activities in this book are designed to be completed at school or at home. You may need to modify the activities and the suggestions below to fit your students' individual needs and your location.

The versatile design of the activity pages allows you to use them in a variety of ways. Here are a few suggestions:

✓ Cut out an activity and duplicate it for each student.

✓ Reproduce an activity as an overhead transparency for the classroom environment.

✓ Duplicate an activity for a take-home project.

✓ Staple the activities together to make an activity book.

✓ Attach each activity to a folder or bin. Place the necessary materials in the folder or bin to have ready when needed.

Materials

Many of the activities call for the use of standard classroom equipment or materials commonly found in the classroom or at home. All of the hands-on activities must be conducted under adult supervision. Always be conscious of safety and emergency procedures.

Assessment

When completing these activities, emphasize the key math vocabulary, concepts, and process skills. After an activity, have students share their answers. During these discussions, have students compare their methods and strategies. Encourage students to ask why a particular mathematical property is true.

4

Math in the Kitchen

The kitchen is an ideal place to discover various math concepts. This unit focuses on the concepts of fractions and of weight. When completing activities in the kitchen environment, make sure students are supervised at all times.

Food provides wonderful opportunities to talk about sharing and simple fractions. It is also an ideal way to discuss the practical applications of weight. Be sure to have plenty of hands-on examples for students.

Concepts

- weight
- ounces
- pounds
- grams
- division
- comparing weight
- using a balance scale
- fractions $\frac{1}{2}$, $\frac{1}{3}$, $\frac{1}{4}$
- sharing

Extension Ideas

- Allow students to explore a food cupboard. Have them observe the weights of different food containers. They should notice the unit used to measure, the actual weight, and if the box feels as heavy as it says it is.

- Have each student decorate a paper plate as a pizza with favorite toppings. Challenge students to cut their pizzas into as many equal pieces as they can and then name the fraction pieces.

Prepare for Activities

✓ various containers of food

✓ paper plates

✓ scissors

✓ crayons

✓ jellybeans

✓ pencil

✓ paper

✓ balance scale

✓ various fruits

✓ I-pound food package

✓ clothes hanger

✓ empty butter tubs

✓ string

✓ For the "Brainy Balancing" activity (page 9), create a homemade balance by hanging a clothes hanger from the ceiling and then hanging an empty tub on each side. The tubs should hang at the same height. Set out containers of various items. Include dried beans, marshmallows, dry cereal, small pasta, etc. Create activity cards. Write "Which weighs MORE?" or "Which weighs LESS?" on each card. Draw two center items on each card. Students will compare the two items by answering the question.

© McGraw-Hill Children's Publishing

0-7682-2901-4 *Math at Home—It's Everyplace You Are*

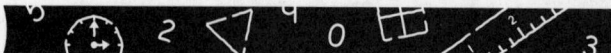

Food Fractions

Directions: Read the word problems.

Answer the questions.

Circle or write your answers.

1. Mary and Sara went out for lunch. They shared a sandwich. They cut it in half. Which fraction shows half?

   a. $\frac{1}{4}$

   b. $\frac{1}{3}$

   c. $\frac{1}{2}$

2. The Ling brothers are sharing doughnuts. There are 3 brothers. There are 3 doughnuts. Which fraction tells what each will get?

   a. one-half

   b. one-third

   c. one-fourth

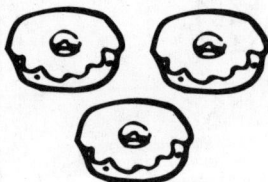

3. A group of 5 friends is sharing a pizza. Each person gets 1 piece. This is $\frac{1}{5}$. Draw lines on the pizza. Show how they cut the pizza.

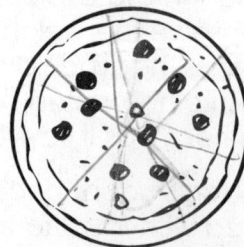

4. Yaron and his friends have 1 cupcake. Each friend gets $\frac{1}{4}$ of the cupcake. Into how many pieces does Yaron cut the cake?

   _____

© McGraw-Hill Children's Publishing

0-7682-2901-4 *Math at Home—It's Everyplace You Are*

What Is Weight?

Directions: Read. Answer the questions. Circle your answer.

Weight tells how heavy something is. Everything has weight. Everything in your home can be weighed.

Weight can be shown in pounds or ounces. Weight can be shown in kilograms or grams.

Where have you seen weight? Maybe you have seen weight on a box of cereal. Food is sometimes weighed in ounces. Maybe you have weighed yourself. People are often weighed in pounds. A frying pan, a small bag of sugar, and a dozen eggs all weigh about a pound.

1. Weight shows how _____ something is.

    a. long

    b. wide

    c. heavy

2. Which can be used to show weight?

    a. meters

    b. grams

    c. liters

3. How are people sometimes weighed?

    a. miles

    b. gallons

    c. pounds

4. How is food sometimes weighed?

    a. ounces

    b. meters

    c. inches

© McGraw-Hill Children's Publishing

0-7682-2901-4 *Math at Home—It's Everyplace You Are*

Paper Plate Fractions

You Need: paper plate, scissors, crayons

Fold a paper plate in half. You have two equal parts. What is one part called? _____

Now fold the plate in half again. You should have four equal parts. What is one part called? _____

Cut out your four equal parts. How many parts equal half a plate? Try it to find out.

Decorate your four parts. They can each be different. Finally, think about foods that start as circles and then are cut into parts.

Sharing Equally

You Need: 6 jellybeans, pencil, paper

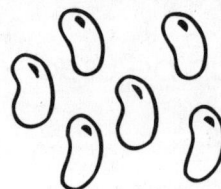

1. Look at your 6 jellybeans. You need to share with 1 person. Make 2 equal piles. Draw your 2 piles. How many jellybeans does each person get? _____3_____

2. Put your 6 jellybeans in 1 pile. Now you need to share with 2 people. Make 3 equal piles. Draw your 3 piles. How many jellybeans does each person get? _____2_____

3. Now eat your jellybeans!

© McGraw-Hill Children's Publishing

0-7682-2901-4 *Math at Home—It's Everyplace You Are*

Brainy Balancing

Go to the balancing center. Choose a card.
Weigh the items shown on the card to find out
how heavy they are. Choose three more cards.
Weigh the items to find out how heavy they are.

Cupboard Hunt

You Need: various containers of food

Look at the food boxes and cans. Can you find how much each
weighs? Look for these words: **ounces**, **pounds**, or **grams**.

Now pick five boxes or cans. Put them in order from heaviest
to lightest.

Now pick five more boxes or cans. Put them in order from lightest
to heaviest.

How do you know they are in the right order?

Putting on the Pounds

You Need: balance scale, 1-pound food package,
various fruits, various containers of food

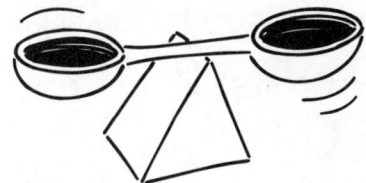

Put the 1-pound package on one side of the scale. Then put one food
on the other side. Keep weighing foods.

Find things that weigh about the same. Put them together.

Find things that weigh more. Put them together.

Find things that weigh less. Put them together.

© McGraw-Hill Children's Publishing

0-7682-2901-4 *Math at Home—It's Everyplace You Are*

Pizza Party

Directions: Color the fractions.

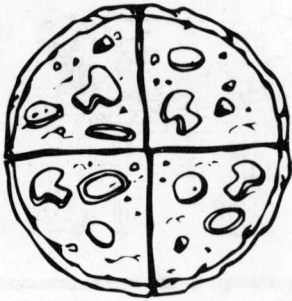

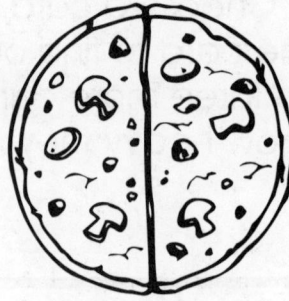

$\frac{1}{4}$

$\frac{1}{2}$

$\frac{1}{3}$

Directions: Draw lines to match.

one-half

$\frac{1}{4}$

$\frac{1}{2}$

one-third

one-fourth

$\frac{1}{3}$

© McGraw-Hill Children's Publishing

0-7682-2901-4 *Math at Home—It's Everyplace You Are*

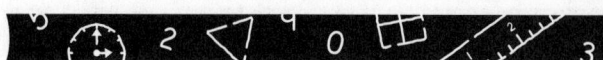

Is It a Pound?

Directions: Look at the picture. What weighs about a pound?

What weighs less than a pound?

Use the code to color.

about a pound = purple	less than a pound = pink
more than a pound = green	

© McGraw-Hill Children's Publishing

0-7682-2901-4 *Math at Home—It's Everyplace You Are*

Math in the Bathroom

Water, water everywhere! This is a great theme for the bathroom. The bathroom is an ideal location to explore volume. Help students understand that containers have capacity and that we can measure and compare capacity. Introduce common customary and metric units, such as cup, pint, quart, gallon, and liter.

Help students measure using objects in the bathroom. Have them use nonstandard and standard units and compare the results.

Concepts
- length
- nonstandard and standard measurement
- metric and customary units
- volume
- comparing volume
- addition and subtraction
- word problems

Prepare for Activities
- ✓ 12-inch ruler
- ✓ pencil
- ✓ centimeter ruler
- ✓ 1-cup measuring cup
- ✓ clean, empty shampoo bottle
- ✓ clean, empty pill bottle
- ✓ small drinking cup
- ✓ empty butter tub
- ✓ paper
- ✓ water
- ✓ 1-gallon jug
- ✓ half-gallon container
- ✓ 1-quart container
- ✓ 1-pint container
- ✓ funnel
- ✓ sink

Extension Idea
- Have students measure their bathrooms using feet. Back in the classroom, give them grid paper that coordinates one-for-one with their feet measurements. Students then draw their bathroom on the grid paper, including large elements such as a counter, a sink, a toilet, and a shower.

© McGraw-Hill Children's Publishing

0-7682-2901-4 *Math at Home—It's Everyplace You Are*

Does It Fit?

Directions: Read and look at the pictures. Answer the questions.

1. Sofi measured the bathroom sink. She wanted a mirror to go above it. Sofi used pencils to measure.

How long is the sink? _____4_____ pencils

2. Aaron measured a bathroom rug.

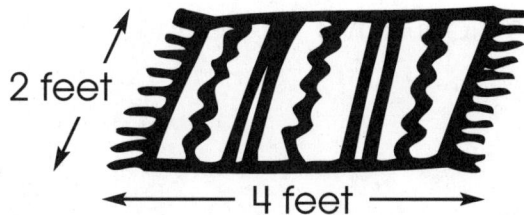

2 feet

4 feet

How long is the rug he bought? _____4_____ feet

3. Sue needs to put a box on the counter. She measures the box.

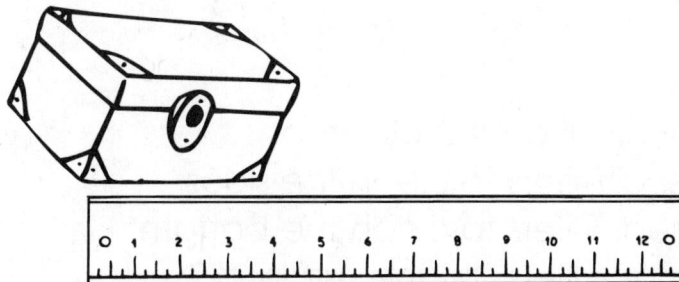

0 1 2 3 4 5 6 7 8 9 10 11 12 0

How long is the box? _____4_____ inches

© McGraw-Hill Children's Publishing   0-7682-2901-4 *Math at Home—It's Everyplace You Are*

Water Problems

Directions: Read and answer the questions.

Volume tells how much a container holds. We can measure volume in many ways.

cups	pints	quarts
gallons	liters	

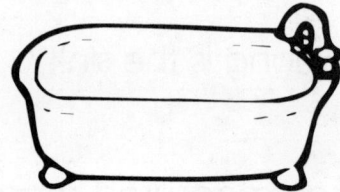

1. Nani was playing in the bathtub.
   She spilled 2 cups of water.
   Her mom cleaned up 1 cup.
   How many cups does Nani have to clean up? ___1 cup___

2. David brushed his teeth.
   He used 1 pint of water.
   Then he washed his face.
   He used 2 pints of water.
   How many pints did he use in all? _____

3. Shelley cleaned the bathtub.
   She used 7 liters to clean the sides.
   She used 3 liters to clean the bottom.
   How many liters did she use in all? _____

© McGraw-Hill Children's Publishing

0-7682-2901-4 *Math at Home—It's Everyplace You Are*

Feet

You Need: 12-inch ruler, pencil

Use your ruler. Measure things around the bathroom. Write the name of each thing where it belongs in the chart.

Shorter than a foot	About a foot	Longer than a foot

How Many Pencils?

You Need: centimeter ruler, pencil, paper

First use a pencil to measure. Then use your ruler.

1. How many ✏️'s wide is your 🚰? _____

2. How many centimeters wide is your 🚰? _____

3. How many ✏️'s long is your 🛁? _____

4. How many centimeters long is your 🛁? _____

5. Find something that is about 8 ✏️'s long. Draw it.

6. Find something that is about 20 cm long. Draw it.

© McGraw-Hill Children's Publishing

0-7682-2901-4 *Math at Home—It's Everyplace You Are*

A Cupful of Guesses

You Need: I-cup measuring cup, clean and empty shampoo bottle, clean and empty pill bottle, small drinking cup, empty butter tub, paper, pencil, water

Look at each thing that can hold water. Do you think each container holds more or less than the measuring cup? Guess. Write the name of the container or draw a picture. Write **more** or **less**.

Now check each guess. Fill the measuring cup with water. Pour water from the cup into each bottle or cup. Does it all fit? Is there room left over? Write **more** or **less**.

Compare the Volume

You Need: I-gallon jug, half-gallon container, I-quart container, I-pint container, I-cup measuring cup, paper, pencil, water, funnel, sink

Work at a sink. Fill the measuring cup with water. Empty water by the cupful into each container. Write down how many cups fill each.

I gallon = _____ cups

half gallon = _____ cups

I quart = _____ cups

I pint = _____ cups

What do you notice? Which containers hold more? How much more do they hold?

© McGraw-Hill Children's Publishing

0-7682-2901-4 *Math at Home—It's Everyplace You Are*

Ruler Rules

Directions: Use your ruler to measure each thing below.

Write your answers in inches and centimeters.

	Inches	Centimeters
1. Length of a toothbrush	in.	cm
2. Height of a shampoo bottle	in.	cm
3. Length of a bar of soap	in.	cm
4. Width of a towel	in.	cm

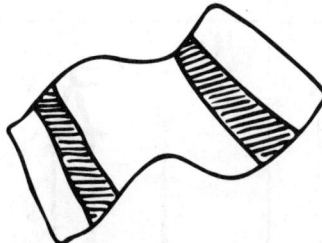

1. Length of a toothbrush

2. Height of a shampoo bottle

3. Length of a bar of soap

4. Width of a towel

5. Find something that is 20 in. Draw it here.

6. Find something that is 3 cm. Draw it here.

© McGraw-Hill Children's Publishing

0-7682-2901-4 *Math at Home—It's Everyplace You Are*

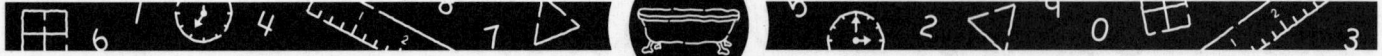

Cups, Pints, and Quarts

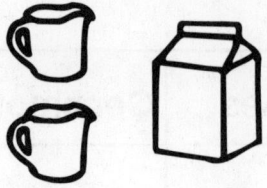  

2 cups = 1 pint   2 pints = 1 quart   4 cups = 1 quart

Directions: Circle which holds **more**.

1.

2.

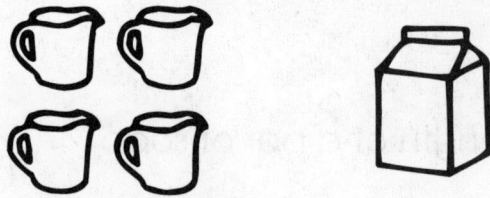

3.

4.

5.

6.

© McGraw-Hill Children's Publishing

0-7682-2901-4 *Math at Home—It's Everyplace You Are*

Math in the Neighborhood

The neighborhood is abundant with different mathematical opportunities. This unit focuses on place value and on mapping. Prior to starting this unit, review the basic concepts of place value. Make sure students understand the meaning of the words *thousands, hundreds, tens,* and *ones*. When introducing students to the concept of maps in a mathematical context, focus on direction, distance, and position. Reinforce commonly used directional words. Encourage students to frequently think about the location and position of items around them.

Concepts

- place value
- writing dollars
- reading maps
- creating maps
- direction
- distance

Prepare for Activities

✓ base-ten blocks

✓ pencil

✓ base-ten block stamps

✓ ink pad

✓ unlined paper

✓ inch ruler

✓ crayons

✓ license plate or license plate number

✓ grid paper

✓ lined paper

Extension Ideas

- Encourage students to notice any places in their neighborhoods where they see numbers. Have them ask "Why are the numbers there?" and "What purpose do they serve?"

- Have students brainstorm about places or times where a map might be useful. What important elements should be on a map and why?

© McGraw-Hill Children's Publishing

0-7682-2901-4 *Math at Home—It's Everyplace You Are*

Going from Place to Place

Directions: Look at the map. Answer the questions.

Circle or write your answers.

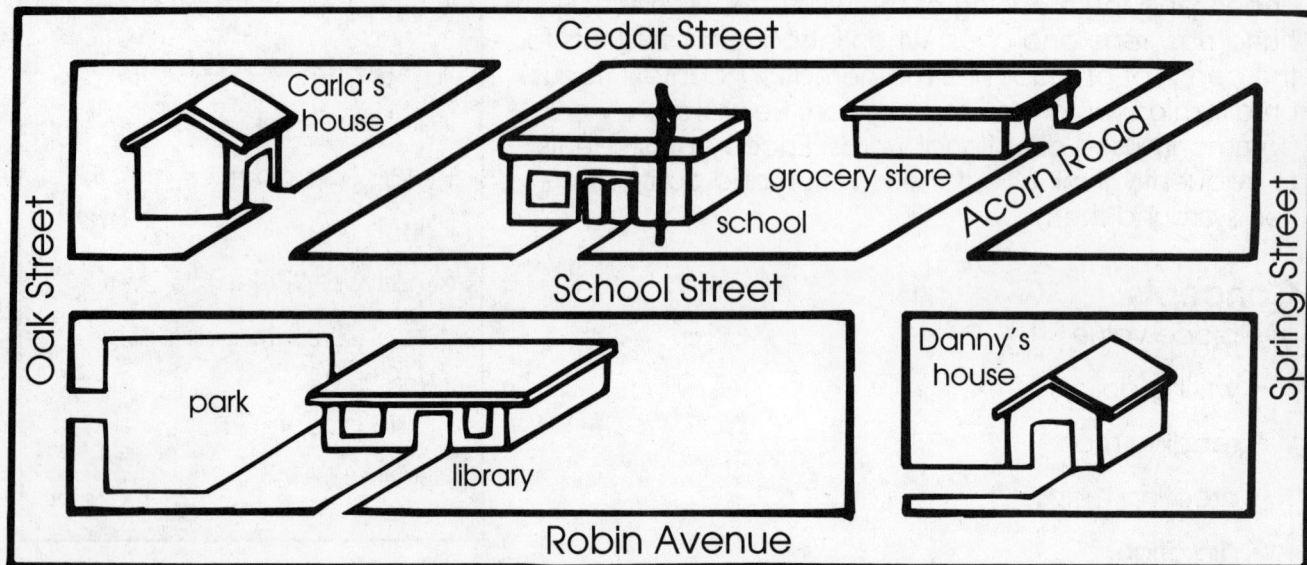

1. What is closest to Danny's house?

   a. Carla's house

   b. grocery store

   c. park

2. What is farthest from Carla's house?

   a. Spring Street

   b. Oak Street

   c. school

3. The park is _____ the library?

   a. far away from

   b. next to

   c. across the street from

© McGraw-Hill Children's Publishing

0-7682-2901-4 *Math at Home—It's Everyplace You Are*

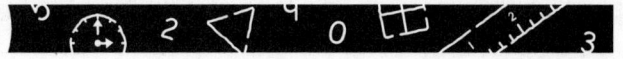

Place Value Riddles

Example: 245

ones
tens
hundreds

Directions: Read the riddles. Write the numbers.

1. I have a 2 in the tens place and a 7 in the ones place.

   Who am I? _____

2. I have a 4 in the ones, tens, and hundreds places.

   Who am I? _____

3. I have no hundreds or tens. I have an 8 in the ones place.

   Who am I? _____

4. I have a 3 in the hundreds place. I have a 0 in the tens place.

   I have a 1 in the ones place.

   Who am I? _____

© McGraw-Hill Children's Publishing

0-7682-2901-4 *Math at Home—It's Everyplace You Are*

Map Your Neighborhood

You Need: unlined paper, pencil, inch ruler, crayons

Key

1 inch = 1 mile

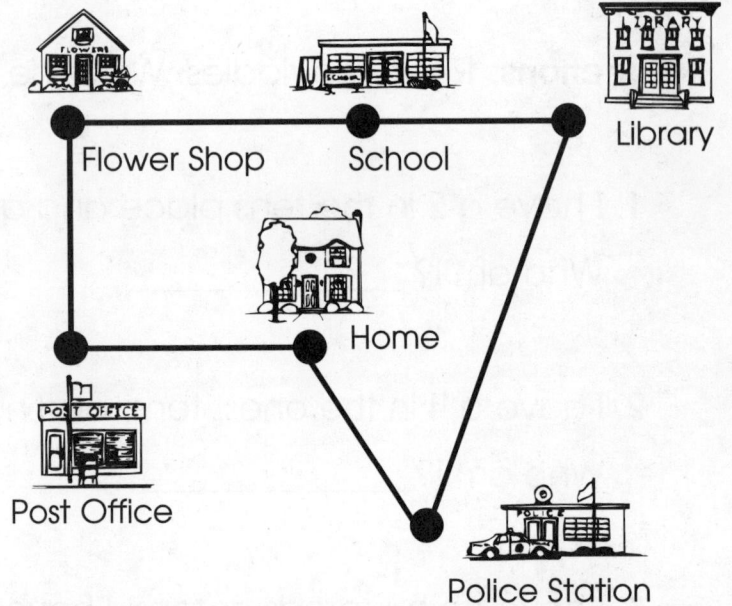

Look at the sample map. Make a map of your own.

First draw your home. Next draw another place like a store or park. Draw a line between your house and the other place.

Make sure the distance is about right. Have 1 inch equal 1 mile. Ask an adult for help.

Make sure you have at least five places on your map.

Flower Shop   School   Library

Home

Post Office

Police Station

Create Your Own Neighborhood

You Need: grid paper, crayons, lined paper, pencil

Use the grid paper to draw a neighborhood. Use your imagination. Include houses, parks, stores, and streets.

Then, write a riddle for a partner. Tell how to get somewhere on your map. Don't tell where, just how. Use street names and directions. Then see if your partner can find the right place.

Direction Words		
right	left	up
down	in front of	behind

© McGraw-Hill Children's Publishing   0-7682-2901-4 *Math at Home—It's Everyplace You Are*

House Number

You Need: base-ten blocks, pencil, paper, base-ten block stamps, ink pad

Each house or apartment has a number. Do you know your house number?

Write your house number. Write how many thousands, hundreds, tens, and ones it has. Show your house number using base-ten blocks. Now stamp your house number using base-ten stamps.

License Plate Numbers

You Need: paper, pencil, license plate

Look at a license plate. It should have numbers. Write down the numbers. The numbers might not be next to each other. Write them down in the order that you see them. Write how many hundreds, tens, and ones.

_____	_____	_____
hundreds	tens	ones

Now write symbols (>, =, <) to compare.

_____	☐	_____
hundreds		tens

_____	☐	_____
hundreds		ones

© McGraw-Hill Children's Publishing

0-7682-2901-4 *Math at Home—It's Everyplace You Are*

© McGraw-Hill Children's Publishing

0-7682-2901-4 *Math at Home—It's Everyplace You Are*

Value of Your House

Directions: Look at the place values. Write the house numbers.

1. 4 hundreds   6 tens   8 ones   =

2. 8 hundreds   5 tens   7 ones   =

Directions: Look at the house numbers.

Write how many hundreds, tens, and ones.

3. **356** = _____ hundreds _____ tens _____ ones

What if your house cost this much? Write the cost in dollars.

_____

4. **742** = _____ hundreds _____ tens _____ ones

What if your house cost this much? Write the cost in dollars.

_____

5. **605** = _____ hundreds _____ tens _____ ones

What if your house cost this much? Write the cost in dollars.

_____

© McGraw-Hill Children's Publishing

0-7682-2901-4 *Math at Home—It's Everyplace You Are*

Math in the Garage

Whether or not students actually have a garage, they can explore with tools, vehicles, sports equipment, and other items commonly found in a garage or car port. There are loads of objects to count, sort, and add or subtract in the garage. Ask students to count and add groups of objects. Encourage students to count objects as they are putting them away. For instance, they could count aluminum cans as they place them in a recycling bin or count the number of steps they take to get to the car.

Have fun in the garage, but be careful. The garage may have dangerous items. This is also a great time to talk about what students may and may not touch.

Concepts
- addition
- subtraction
- sorting
- classifying

Extension Ideas
- Count and add things in the garage, but be more specific. Have students count objects that are used to take care of the yard, tools that fix the car, sports equipment, things that move, etc. Have students make statements about which group has more or less and what looks different about each group.

- Gather sets of safe tools, such as children's plastic tools or simple objects like clean paintbrushes and gardening gloves. Have students sort them into piles by size, color, or use.

Prepare for Activities
- ✓ various screws and nails
- ✓ muffin tin
- ✓ paper scraps
- ✓ crayons
- ✓ pencil
- ✓ paper
- ✓ various balls and outdoor toys
- ✓ For the "Sort It!" activity (page 29), provide students with a variety of screws and nails. Include flat and Phillips head, different colors, and different sizes. Students will choose how to sort and then sort into a muffin tin.

© McGraw-Hill Children's Publishing

0-7682-2901-4 *Math at Home—It's Everyplace You Are*

Sorting It Out

Directions: Read and answer the questions.

1. Sonya sorted her tools.

She sorted garden tools and regular tools.

Garden: gloves, watering can, trowel

Regular: hammer, wrench, saw, rake

What did Sonya do wrong? _____

Write or draw one more tool that could go in each.

Garden: _____

Regular: _____

2. Rick sorted his toys.

Look at his set.

Set 1
bike
inline skates
scooter

Set 2
basketball
jump rope
kite

How did Rick sort? _____

Write a title for each set.

Set 1: _____

Set 2: _____

© McGraw-Hill Children's Publishing

0-7682-2901-4 *Math at Home—It's Everyplace You Are*

In the Garage

Directions: Read and answer the questions. Use the pictures to
help you solve.

1. Claudio found 3 screwdrivers and 4 hammers.

   How many tools did he find in all? _____

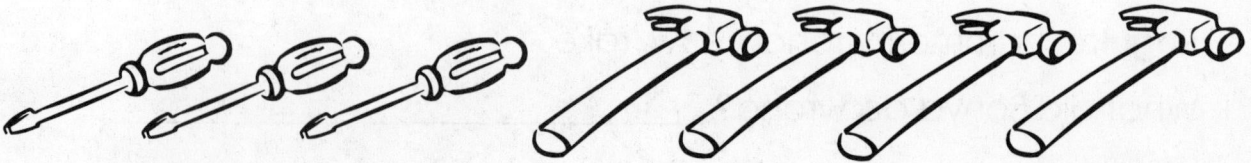

2. Tanya had 6 tennis balls. The dog chewed up 2.

   How many balls does she have now? _____

3. Raquel found 2 things to clean with. She found 2 things to build with.

   How many things did she find in all? _____

4. Jamal had a box of 10 nails. He dropped 3 nails and lost them.

   How many things does he have now? _____

© McGraw-Hill Children's Publishing   0-7682-2901-4 *Math at Home—It's Everyplace You Are*

Sort It!

You Need: various screws and nails, muffin tin, paper scraps, crayons

Look at the objects. How will you sort them? You might sort by size, shape, or color.

Use crayons and paper to make labels. Place one label by each muffin cup.

Now sort the objects.

After you have sorted, take the labels off the tin. Work with a partner. Can your partner guess how you sorted?

Sport Sort

You Need: various balls and outdoor toys

Look at the toys.

Sort the toys by shape. Which toy is the largest in each shape pile? Do any toys not match a shape?

Sort the toys by size. Use small, medium, and large. Does the size help you play with a toy?

Sort the toys by color. Is the color important to the toy?

© McGraw-Hill Children's Publishing

0-7682-2901-4 *Math at Home—It's Everyplace You Are*

Garage Hunt

You Need: pencil, paper

Look in your garage. Find and count the following.

1. tools _____

2. toys _____

3. cars _____

Answer the questions. Use a calculator if the numbers are too big.

4. How many tools and toys are there altogether? _____

5. How many tools and cars are there altogether? _____

6. How many things are there in all? _____

Write Your Own

You Need: pencil, paper, crayons

Write your own story problems. Use addition or subtraction. Your story problems must take place in a garage.

Write two problems. Draw pictures to help. Have a partner solve the problems.

© McGraw-Hill Children's Publishing

0-7682-2901-4 *Math at Home—It's Everyplace You Are*

Jackie's Sort

Set 1

Set 2

1. How did Jackie sort her toys?

    a. outdoor and indoor toys

    b. toys with balls and other toys

    c. round toys and square toys

2. How many more toys are in Set 1 than Set 2? _____

3. Draw one more toy in each set.

© McGraw-Hill Children's Publishing

0-7682-2901-4 *Math at Home—It's Everyplace You Are*

Bouncing Balls

Directions: Help clean the garage. Pick up the balls.

Solve each problem. You will add or subtract.

1.
$$\begin{array}{r} 10 \\ -\ 7 \\ \hline \end{array}$$

2.
$$\begin{array}{r} 4 \\ +\ 3 \\ \hline \end{array}$$

3.
$$\begin{array}{r} 6 \\ -\ 3 \\ \hline \end{array}$$

4.
$$\begin{array}{r} 0 \\ +\ 9 \\ \hline \end{array}$$

5.
$$\begin{array}{r} 7 \\ +\ 1 \\ \hline \end{array}$$

6.
$$\begin{array}{r} 8 \\ -\ 5 \\ \hline \end{array}$$

7.
$$\begin{array}{r} 10 \\ -\ 1 \\ \hline \end{array}$$

8.
$$\begin{array}{r} 2 \\ +\ 2 \\ \hline \end{array}$$

© McGraw-Hill Children's Publishing

0-7682-2901-4 *Math at Home—It's Everyplace You Are*

Math on the Porch

The porch, patio, deck, balcony, and front stoop are all great places to practice with data analysis and time. Students can sit and observe objects, people, and the environment without having to go on an involved field trip. Encourage students to notice how things grow, change, move, and stay the same throughout the day, week, month, and year. Specifically, relate what they already know about time to the physical characteristics of different times of the day.

Concepts

- bar graph
- weather
- pictograph
- tally chart
- sun dial
- frequency
- time
- time of day
- measurement

Extension Idea

- Have students create other kinds of graphs after observing how long the grass grows in a week, how many people pass the house in a 15-minute time period, or other measurable observations.

Prepare for Activities

✓ construction paper

✓ crayons

✓ clothespins

✓ clear plastic cups

✓ permanent markers

✓ centimeter ruler

✓ white paper

✓ tag board

✓ cardboard

✓ pencil

✓ large cardboard squares

✓ For the "Make a Sundial" activity (page 37), cut out an 8-inch (20 cm) circle from tag board for each student.

✓ For the "Kiddy Clock" activity (page 37), help students create a large outdoor clock as described on page 37. Choose a student to start first. That student will stand in the middle of the clock. Ask the other students what time they might do a common daily activity, such as brushing their teeth. Once a time is selected, the student inside the clock must lie down and use his or her arms and legs to model correct clock hand position for that time. Allow each student time in the clock. Be sure to include hours and half-hours.

33

Joel's Graph

Joel lives in a house by the airport. Each day he sits on his deck. He can hear the planes. They fly right over his house.

Joel wrote down how many planes flew over the house. Then he made a pictograph.

Airplane Flights

Monday	✈ ✈
Tuesday	✈ ✈ ✈ ✈
Wednesday	✈ ✈ ✄
Thursday	✈ ✈
Friday	✈ ✈ ✈ ✈ ✈ ✄

✈ = 2 flights

Directions: Answer the questions about Joel's graph.

1. How many flights were there on Monday and Tuesday?

   _____

2. How many more flights were there on Wednesday than on Thursday?

   _____

3. How many flights were there on Tuesday? _____

4. What was the total number of flights all week? _____

© McGraw-Hill Children's Publishing

0-7682-2901-4 *Math at Home—It's Everyplace You Are*

Time of Day

Directions: Write the number from the right picture to answer the questions.

1

2

3

4

1. When do you ? _____

2. When do you ? _____

3. When do you ? _____

4. When do you ? _____

5. When do you ? _____

6. When do you ? _____

© McGraw-Hill Children's Publishing

0-7682-2901-4 *Math at Home—It's Everyplace You Are*

Weather Graph

You Need: construction paper, crayons, 7 clothespins

Make a weather recording chart. Divide a piece of construction paper into four equal parts. In each part, draw pictures to show sunny, rainy, windy, and cloudy.

Go onto your porch, deck, or balcony to look at the weather. Each day, clip a clothespin onto your chart to show the weather. Do this for one week.

Now create a bar graph. Have an adult help you. Show the number of days. Use bars to show how many days had each kind of weather.

Measuring Rain

You Need: clear plastic cup, permanent marker, paper, crayons, rain, centimeter ruler

Start at the bottom of your plastic cup. Measure up 5 cm. Draw a line. Keep doing this until you hit the top of the cup. Place your cup outside in a place where it can't be knocked over.

Measure how much rain falls into the cup each day for five days. Look at the cup from the side. Read how many centimeters.

Now create a pictograph. Draw a graph. Use raindrop shapes to show how many centimeters of rain fell each day.

© McGraw-Hill Children's Publishing

0-7682-2901-4 *Math at Home—It's Everyplace You Are*

Make a Sundial

You Need: tag board circle, pencil

A sundial is a way to tell time. Pretend your circle is a clock. Write the clock numbers around the circle. Draw a dot in the middle of the circle. Take your clock outside. Lay the clock on the ground. Push a stick through the dot in the center and into the ground.

Check your clock every hour. Draw a mark to show where the shadow is. Then bring the clock inside. Look at your marks. Does the sun really tell time?

Kiddy Clock

You Need: large cardboard squares, markers

Write the numbers of the clock on the cardboard squares. Go outside to a deck or grassy area. Lay the numbers down in a circle. Make a big clock.

Listen to your teacher. She will have a classmate tell you a time. You will lie on your back in the clock. Use your arms and legs to show the time.

What Do You Do?

You Need: pencil, paper

Look at each time of day below. What do you do at that time? Write two things for each time of day.

_____ _____ _____ _____

_____ _____ _____ _____

© McGraw-Hill Children's Publishing

0-7682-2901-4 *Math at Home—It's Everyplace You Are*

Sunny Skies

Directions: The pictures show the weather for one month. Look at the number of sunny, cloudy, and rainy days there were.

IIII IIII IIII IIII   IIII IIII IIII IIII   IIII IIII

IIII IIII

Directions: Create a pictograph using the data above.

Weather for One Month

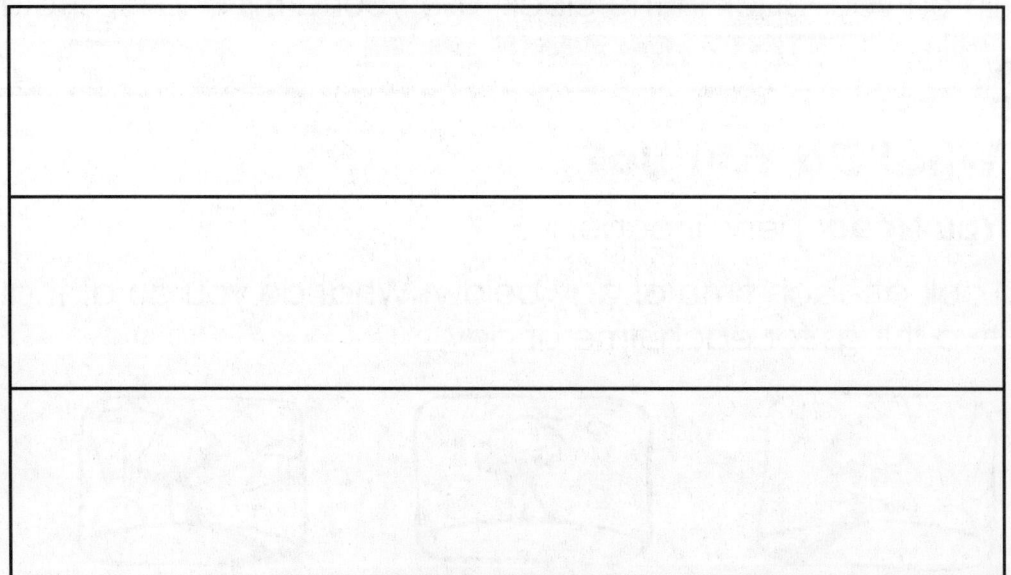

Number of Days

© McGraw-Hill Children's Publishing

0-7682-2901-4 *Math at Home—It's Everyplace You Are*

My Busy Day

Directions: Cut out the clocks. Look at each picture.

Glue the clock that shows the right time for each activity.

Go to School	Lunch and Recess
Breakfast	Dinner
Wake Up	Bedtime

7:00 A.M.	8:00 A.M.	9:00 A.M.	12:00 NOON	6:00 P.M.	8:00 P.M.

© McGraw-Hill Children's Publishing

0-7682-2901-4 *Math at Home—It's Everyplace You Are*

Math in Other Places at Home

Allow students to explore math throughout the house. The living room, bedroom, dining room, basement, and attic all contain items that can be used to teach math.

This unit focuses on patterns and shapes, which often go hand-in-hand. Challenge students to see flat and 3-D shapes in everything that they use during the day. Also challenge them to see patterns in objects, sounds, and actions that they encounter on a daily basis.

Concepts

- recognizing patterns
- extending patterns
- creating patterns
- shapes (flat and 3-D)
- shapes in everyday objects

Extension Ideas

- Students should keep a log of shapes and patterns that they find throughout their homes and at school. Encourage students to either write about what they see or draw pictures to record. Discuss why patterns or shapes are important to what they see.

- Purchase plain white T-shirts and puffy washable fabric paint. Have students practice drawing a pattern on scrap paper. Then let them use the fabric paint to apply their patterns to the T-shirts.

Prepare for Activities

✓ crayons

✓ plastic bags

✓ macaroni

✓ powdered tempera paint

✓ paper towels

✓ plastic needles

✓ heavy thread

✓ pencil

✓ For the "Shape Chase" activity (page 44), create large cards with images of common flat shapes. Arrange students around the room. You will flash a card. Students must find three objects of that shape, touch them, and return back to their original spots. Observe the objects students touch and discuss.

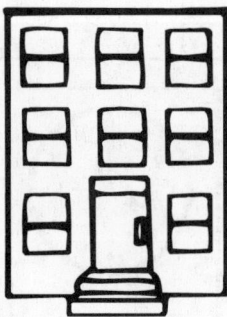

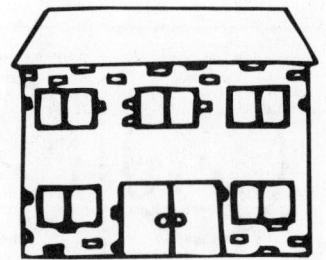

© McGraw-Hill Children's Publishing

What Are Patterns?

Directions: Read and answer the questions.

A pattern is something that repeats. A pattern must have more than one part. The parts are in a special order.

A pattern can use shapes. This is a shape pattern:

★ ♥ ★ ♥ ★ ♥ ★ ♥

1. How many parts are in this pattern? _____

A pattern can use letters. This is a letter pattern:

A B C A B C A B C A B C

2. How many parts are in this pattern? _____

A pattern can use numbers. This is a number pattern:

1 2 2 1 2 2 1 2 2 1 2 2

3. How many parts are in this pattern? _____

Look for patterns at home. You can see patterns on clothes, curtains, and walls. Floors, dishes, and books might also have patterns.

© McGraw-Hill Children's Publishing

0-7682-2901-4 *Math at Home—It's Everyplace You Are*

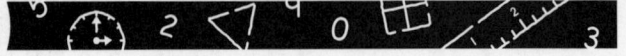
Shape Riddles

Directions: Use the clues to guess each shape. Draw a line to the right shape. Then write the name of the shape on the line.

cube	cylinder	rectangle
circle	sphere	

1. I am a three-dimensional shape. I have curved sides. I have no edges. Who am I?

   _____

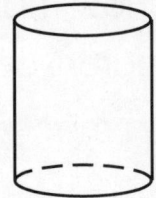

2. I am a flat shape. I have four sides. My sides are not all equal. Who am I?

   _____

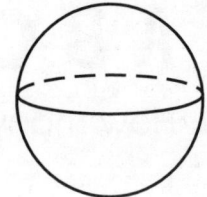

3. I am a three-dimensional shape. I have six sides. Each side is a square. Who am I?

   _____

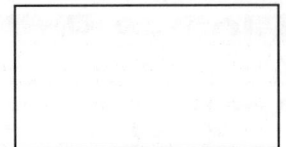

4. I am a flat shape. I have no sides. Who am I?

   _____

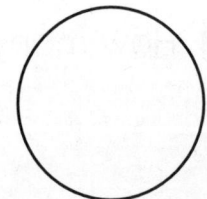

5. I am a three-dimensional shape. Two of my sides are circles. Who am I?

   _____

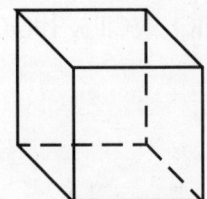

© McGraw-Hill Children's Publishing

0-7682-2901-4 *Math at Home—It's Everyplace You Are*

Bead Patterns

You Need: plastic bags, macaroni, powdered tempera paint, paper towels, plastic needle threaded with heavy thread

Jewelry often has a pattern. Sometimes the pattern uses color, shape, or size.

Make your own jewelry pattern. Place pasta in bags. Add different colored tempera paint. Close bags and shake. Shake off excess powder and place macaroni on paper towels.

String macaroni together with a needle and thread. Create a pattern using at least two different colors. Keep threading until the necklace is as long as you want it. Tie the ends of the string together in a triple knot.

Tell about the pattern using words. Write the pattern using letters.

Clothes Patterns

You Need: pencil

Look at the scarf.

Tell about the pattern using words.

Write the pattern using letters.

Look at the tie.

Tell about the pattern using words.

Write the pattern using numbers.

© McGraw-Hill Children's Publishing

0-7682-2901-4 *Math at Home—It's Everyplace You Are*

Familiar Shapes

You Need: pencil

What shape is this ball? _____

Name something that has the same shape. _____

What shape is this block? _____

Name something else that has the same shape. _____

What shape is this garbage can? _____

Name something else that has the same shape. _____

Shape Chase

You Need: set of shape cards

Stand around the room with other students. Your teacher will show one shape card. Look at the shape. Find three things in the room that are the same shape. Touch each thing. Then move back to where you started.

© McGraw-Hill Children's Publishing

0-7682-2901-4 *Math at Home—It's Everyplace You Are*

Coloring Patterns

I. Color the stripes on the sweater. Use a green, orange pattern.

2. Draw a stripe, zigzag pattern on the mitten.

3. Color the quilt. Follow the pattern. Choose your own colors.

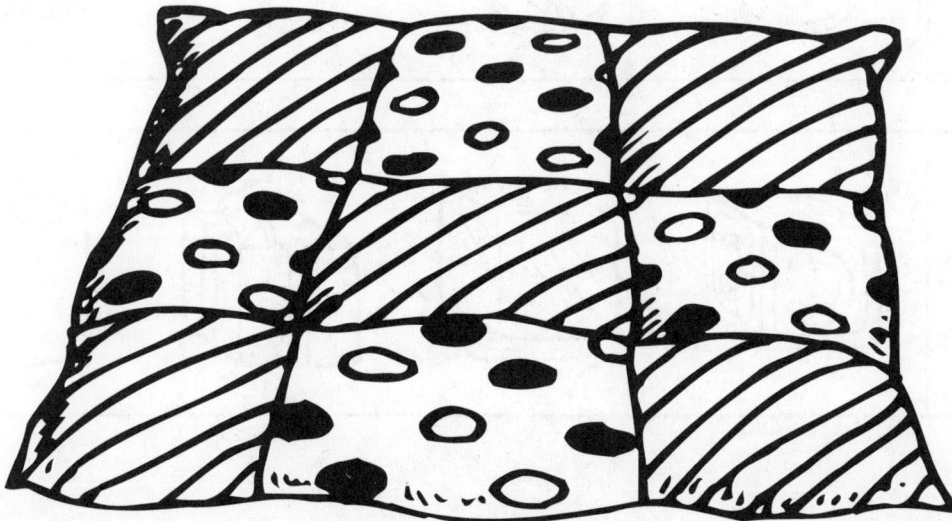

© McGraw-Hill Children's Publishing

0-7682-2901-4 *Math at Home—It's Everyplace You Are*

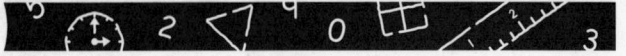

Household Objects

Directions: Look at each row.

Draw an **X** on the one that does not belong.

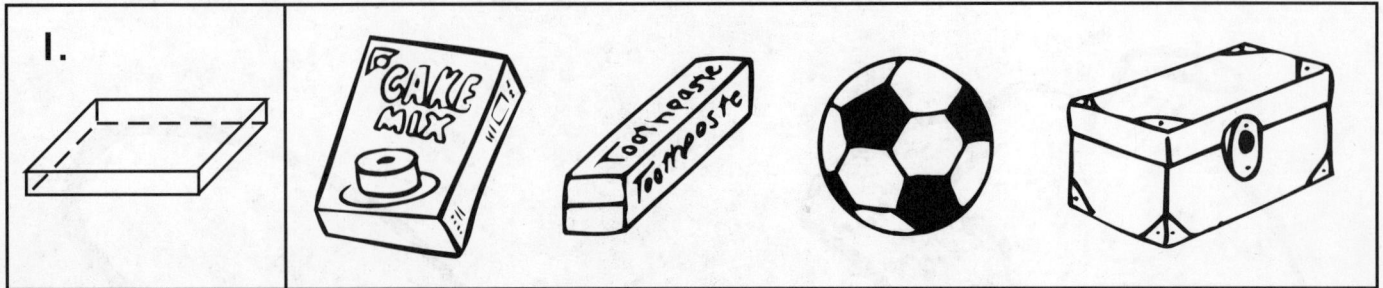

1.

2.

3.

4.

© McGraw-Hill Children's Publishing

0-7682-2901-4 *Math at Home—It's Everyplace You Are*

Vocabulary

3-D shape—three-dimensional shape; a figure that has length, width, and height

bar graph—a graph that uses bars related to a number scale to show data

base-ten—a number system in which each digit has ten times the value of the same digit one place to its right

base-ten blocks—blocks showing increments of 1,000s, 100s, 10s, and 1s

base-ten block stamps—rubber stamps depicting base-ten blocks (available from McGraw-Hill Children's Publishing)

compare—describe as similar or different

directional words—words that convey direction, such as *left*, *right*, *in front of*, and *behind*

estimate—a guess that is close to the exact answer

flat shape—a figure with only one dimension

half—one part of a whole that has been divided into two equal parts

NCTM—National Council of Teachers of Mathematics

NCTM standards—the most recently published guidelines from the NCTM that explain the math learning expectations for students

nonstandard—a measure that does not use the customary or metric notation

part—a portion of a whole object, amount, or group

pattern—a series of numbers or figures that follows a repeating rule

pictograph—a graph that uses repeated images to show data

place value—the value of a digit within a number, determined by its position

tally chart—a chart that uses tally marks to record amount

volume—the amount of space inside a container

© McGraw-Hill Children's Publishing

0-7682-2901-4 *Math at Home—It's Everyplace You Are*

Answer Key

Food Fractions . . . . . . Page 6
1. c
2. b
3. Pizza should be cut into 5 equal pieces.
4. 4 pieces

What Is Weight? . . . . . Page 7
1. c
2. b
3. c
4. a

Paper Plate Fractions. . Page 8
$\frac{1}{2}$, $\frac{1}{4}$, 2

Sharing Equally . . . . . . Page 8
1. 3 jellybeans
2. 2 jellybeans

Pizza Party. . . . . Page 10
pizza in three pieces—
one-third—$\frac{1}{3}$
pizza in 4 pieces—
one-fourth—$\frac{1}{4}$
pizza in 2 pieces—
one-half—$\frac{1}{2}$

Is It a Pound? . . . . . . Page 11
Purple: plant, box, jug, chair, cereal bowl
Pink: apple, glass, napkin, paper and pencil, vase, hat, cat food bowl
Green: table, dog, cat

Does It Fit? . . . . Page 13
1. 4 pencils
2. 4 feet
3. 4 inches

Water Problems . . . . Page 14
1. 1 cup
2. 3 pints
3. 10 liters

Ruler Rules . . . . Page 17
Answers will vary.

Cups, Pints, and Quarts . . . . Page 18
1. quart
2. 4 cups
3. 5 cups
4. 3 pints
5. 6 cups
6. pint

Going from Place to Place . . . . Page 20
1. b
2. a
3. b

Place Value Riddles . . . . Page 21
1. 27
2. 444
3. 8
4. 301

Value of Your House. . . . . Page 25
1. 468
2. 857
3. 3 hundreds, 5 tens, 6 ones; $356.00
4. 7 hundreds, 4 tens, 2 ones; $742.00
5. 6 hundreds, 0 tens, 5 ones; $605.00

Sorting It Out. . . . . . . Page 27
1. She put the rake with the regular tools.; Answers will vary.
2. Toys with Wheels and Other Toys; Answers will vary.

In the Garage. . . . . . Page 28
1. 7
2. 4
3. 4
4. 7

Jackie's Sort . . . . . . Page 31
1. b
2. 2 more
3. Students should draw a ball in Set 1 and a toy that is not a ball in Set 2.

Bouncing Balls . . . . . Page 32
1. 3
2. 7
3. 3
4. 9
5. 8
6. 3
7. 9
8. 4

Joel's Graph . . . . . . Page 34
1. 12
2. 1
3. 8
4. 32

Time of Day. . . . . Page 35
1. 1
2. 2
3. 4
4. 2
5. 1
6. 4

Sunny Skies. . . . . Page 38
Graph should show 15 suns, 10 clouds, and 5 umbrellas.

My Busy Day. . . . . . . Page 39
Order of clocks, left to right and top to bottom is: 9:00, 12:00, 8:00 A.M., 6:00, 7:00, and 8:00 P.M.

What Are Patterns? . . Page 41
1. 2 parts
2. 3 parts
3. 2 parts

Shape Riddles. . . . . . . Page 42
1. sphere
2. rectangle
3. cube
4. circle
5. cylinder

Coloring Patterns . . . Page 45
1. Stripes on sweater should alternate green, orange in a pattern.
2. Mitten should have a stripe, zigzag pattern that repeats.
3. Quilt should be colored using a two-color pattern to match the design.

Household Objects. . Page 46
1. soccer ball
2. chocolate bar
3. piece of pie
4. toilet paper roll

48

© McGraw-Hill Children's Publishing

0-7682-2901-4 *Math at Home—It's Everyplace You Are*